First published by Candlewick Press

CANDLEWICK PRESS
2067 MASSACHUSETTS AVENUE
CAMBRIDGE MA 02140

ISBN 0-590-62942-5

Text copyright © 1994 by Foxbusters Ltd. Illustrations copyright © 1994 by Anita Jeram. All rights reserved. Published by Scholastic Inc., 555 Broadway, New York, NY 10012, by arrangement with Candlewick Press.

12 11 10 9 8 7 6 5 4   7 8 9/9 0 1/0

Printed in the U.S.A.   08

First Scholastic printing, January 1996

I LOVE GUINEA PIGS

by

Dick King-Smith

illustrated by

Anita Jeram

CANDLEWICK PRESS

CAMBRIDGE, MASSACHUSETTS

There's a silly old saying that
if you hold a guinea pig up
by its tail, its eyes
will drop out.

Well of course they wouldn't,

even if you could—which you couldn't,

because guinea pigs don't have tails.

And they aren't pigs either.

They're rodents—like mice and rats
and squirrels.

As for the other part of their name, guinea pigs were first brought to Europe about four hundred years ago by Spanish sailors, probably from a country in South America called Dutch Guiana. And the sailors called them "guiana pigs."

In fact, the guinea pig is a member of the cavy family, and its Latin name is *Cavia porcellus* (which means a piggy-looking cavy).

Anyway, whatever they're called,

it's the way they look that I've

always liked. They're so

chunky and chubby

and cuddly, with their blunt

heads and sturdy bodies and short legs.

smooth

Peruvian

crested

They come in tons of different colors, and
they can be smooth-coated or rough-coated
or long-coated, not to mention
the other varieties.
I've had hundreds of
guinea pigs over the last fifty years,
but I've always liked the Abyssinians best.

sheltie

Abyssinians

Guinea pigs are such sensible animals.

They're awfully easy to keep,

because they aren't fussy.

They don't like the cold, of
course, or the damp, any more
than you would, and they're not happy living
in a poky little place, any more than
you would be. But as long as they have
a comfortable, warm, dry place to live,
guinea pigs are as happy as can be.

Guinea pigs like a really big roomy hutch or,
better still, a wire pen out on the grass.

They're hardy animals and don't often get sick. Properly cared for, they can live a long time.

Most guinea pigs live for about five to eight years.

I once had a crested sow
named Zen. She lived two years
with me and then eight more
with one of my daughters.
People's hair grows whiter
as they age, but Zen's
grew darker.

Guinea pigs need
plenty of food.

They love eating, just like you do, and feeding

them is half the fun of having them.

Some people, of course, feed them

nothing but hay and pellets from

the pet store, and they're just fine.

But how boring a diet like that must

be, both for the piggy-looking

cavy and its

owner.

I always used to give my
guinea pigs lots of other kinds of
food as well: cabbage and cauliflower leaves,
carrots, pieces of bread and apple peelings, and
wild plants, like dandelions
and clover. I gave them
water, too, of course.

Guinea pigs need
clean drinking
water every day. And their water
bottle often needs washing,
because they like blowing pieces
of food back up the spout.

One especially nice thing
about guinea pigs is that
if you handle them
regularly, and carry them around, stroke
them, talk to them, and make a fuss
over them, they become
really fond of you.

The correct way to pick up
a guinea pig is with one hand
over its shoulders and the other
supporting its bottom.

Another nice thing about
guinea pigs is that they
talk a lot.

When they want food or water,

they often give a sort of whistle,

sometimes low,

sometimes loud.

Boars say *chutter* when
they're squaring up
for a fight.

So do sows when their babies
pester them too much.

Other things guinea pigs say are

putt

chut

tweet

and *drr*.

But when one guinea pig says *purr* to another
guinea pig, it's as plain as the nose on your face
that it only means one thing:

"I love you."

And that brings me to
what's best of all about
having guinea pigs—baby ones.
Because their ancestors, the wild cavies
of South America, lived out in the
open with enemies all around them,
their young ones had to be
ready to run for it.

So the guinea pig sow carries her unborn litter for a very long time, about seventy days, and they arrive in the world fully furred, with their eyes open and their mouths already filled with teeth.

Newborn guinea pigs are such a comical sight. Their heads and feet look too big for their bodies.

Baby rabbits are born blind and naked and helpless, but not baby guinea pigs.

But almost immediately

they show an interest in those two

favorite guinea pig pursuits—

eating

and conversation.

Of all the guinea pigs I've had,
there were two that I will never
forget. Both were Abyssinians,
both were boars, and each in his
time fathered dozens of lovely
big-headed, big-footed babies.

One was a bright golden color,
and his name was King Arthur.
The other was a blue roan named
Beach Boy. Both are buried in
my yard.

There's a solitary apple tree at the edge
of my lawn, and I like to look at it and think
that under it Beach Boy and King Arthur
lie peacefully, one on one side of the tree,
one on the other.

I'm not sad about this—
just happy to remember
what a lot of pleasure
I've had from all
my guinea pigs.

One especially nice
thing about guinea pigs
is that if you make a fuss
over them, they become
really fond of you.